# Hard Times

# BOOKS IN THE PROTESTANT PULPIT EXCHANGE

Be My People: Sermons on the Ten Commandments
*Ross W. Marrs*

Be My Guest: Sermons on the Lord's Supper
*C. Thomas Hilton*

Believe in Me: Sermons on the Apostles' Creed
*James A. Harnish*

Fatal Attractions: Sermons on the Seven Deadly Sins
*William R. White*

What Are You Waiting For?
Sermons on the Parables of Jesus
*Mark Trotter*

Ripe Life: Sermons on the Fruit of the Spirit
*C. Thomas Hilton*

Pack Up Your Troubles: Sermons on How to Trust in God
*Maxie Dunnam*

# Hard Times

## Sermons on Hope

### Donna Schaper

PROTESTANT
PULPIT
EXCHANGE

Abingdon Press
Nashville

# HARD TIMES: SERMONS ON HOPE

*Copyright © 1993 by Abingdon Press*

*This book is printed on recycled, acid-free paper.*

**Library of Congress Cataloging-in-Publication Data**

Schaper, Donna.
    Hard times : sermons on hope / Donna Schaper.
       p.    cm. — (Protestant pulpit exchange)
    **ISBN 0-687-37559-2** (alk. paper)
    1. Hope—Religious aspects—Christianity—Sermons. 2. Sermons, American.
I. Series.
BV4638.S3253    1993
234'.2—dc20
                                       93-4028
                                          CIP

Scripture quotations, unless otherwise noted, are from the New Revised Standard Version of the Bible, copyright © 1989 by the Division of Christian Education of the National Council of the Churches of Christ in the USA. Used by permission.

Scripture quotations marked RSV are from the Revised Standard Version of the Bible copyright © 1946, 1952, 1971 by the Division of Christian Education of the National Council of the Churches of Christ in the USA. Used by permission.

Scripture quotations marked Moffatt are from *The Bible: A New Translation* by James Moffatt. Copyright © 1954 by James Moffatt.

Scripture quotations marked KJV are from the King James Version of the Bible.

The sermon "Hope for the Elder Brother" is a revision of sermons originally published in *Salt* and *Kairos* magazines.

93 94 95 96 97 98 99 00 01 02 — 10 9 8 7 6 5 4 3 2 1

MANUFACTURED IN THE UNITED STATES OF AMERICA

*To Hazel Harrup,*
*who hoped enough*
*to risk a lot at age eighty-six*

# Contents

# Introduction

ope is the place we go when optimism fails. Right now the times are hard. Few people are optimistic about the economy or the environment or the culture: we fear for our jobs, for the ozone layer, for the manners of our children. Fear is the national pastime. Optimism is on vacation. The slate is cleared for hope.

We are at a time of great cultural conversion, not great cultural catastrophe. Those of us who feel like we are stuck to moral flypaper—unable to fly until "things settle down"—are eager to awaken our hope, what the poet Emily Dickinson calls "that thing with feathers."

To those still seduced by the data, hope seems like a luxury. We misunderstand its relationship to optimism. Hope is not based in the evidence and is not damaged when the evidence disappears. Hope instead gets stronger in darker times. Hope is less the belief that things are going to turn out well than it is the confidence that, no matter how

9

things turn out, they still make sense and carry meaning. Hope is believing in God's promises more than we are seduced by those of the world.

Because hope is not based on the facts, it can actually thrive in the face of genuine danger. The child stuck at the bottom of a well is not optimistic; she hopes. The adult who assesses the possibility of nuclear danger realistically does not indulge fantasy; he hopes. Likewise the man who has lost his job reads the classified ads with hope, not wishful thinking. Hope is that thing that gets people who have lost their reason to get out of bed in the morning, out of bed in the morning. Hope thrives in hard times.

Christopher Lasch, the historian, says it well when he says:

> We need to recover a more vigorous form of hope, which trusts life without denying its tragic character or attempting to explain away tragedy as "cultural lag." We can fully appreciate this kind of hope only now that the other kind, better described as optimism, has fully revealed itself as a higher form of wishful thinking. (*The True and Only Heaven* [New York: W. W. Norton, 1991], p. 37)

What follows is an examination of hope from the perspective of a few selected biblical texts. There are people who say that the entire theme of the gospel is hope, and they are probably right. The Old Testament sees hope as waiting for the Messiah and the promised time. For good examples, see Psalm 62:1-5 or 130:1-6 or probably the most famous one, Isaiah 40:29-31. The New Testament sees it as living in the realized promised time—as though it were already here—through the death and resurrection of Jesus Christ. This gospel is at least the invitation—what Douglas John Hall calls the permission and the command—to enter trouble hopefully. It is the way we live in God's future and not the world's present, without abandoning the world to itself. We wait on the Lord when we can't see or feel or acknowledge the Lord—and we also watch the Lord at work in a present that appears, at first glance, not to be a realized promise.

Asked by a younger woman when she could expect to live with the degree of courage and insight that the older woman was living by, the old woman responded, "When you have lost as many things as I have and found them all again" (Susan O'Halloran and Susan Delotte, *The Woman Who Lost Her Heart* [San Diego: Luramedia, 1992], p. 81). Hope waits through the loss. Hope lives as though the loss were simply the first meaning of the larger meaning revealed. Hope looks for the Christ in the crucifixion.

"By the way they live, most people fuel their belief in the terror of living. It takes great courage to finish your life larger than when you began. It requires deep trust to take action, to open and to grow" (*The Woman Who Lost Her Heart,* p. 86). The wise woman who helped the girl find her heart speaks again. Especially when we are called to live in hard times, we refuse the invitation to grow. Trust becomes more than normally difficult. When the trust to take action and to open and to grow leaves us, there is too little opening for hope to get through. That's why hope does have friends in trust and faith; they are the feet it dangles in the water.

Oscar Romero said, "If you need to feel hope you're courting despair, and if you court despair you'll stop working. . . . Try to have faith instead, to do what you can, and stop worrying about whether or not you're effective. Worry about what is possible for you to do, which is always greater than you can imagine." Romero is surely right about the penchant for privileged people like myself to need more guarantees about the water's temperature before we swim. I have found that I do worry about hope. I do refuse to take first steps until I get insurance for second steps. This work on hope acknowledges the role of trust and faith but talks to privileged people about the insurance policy that both testaments promise. It does so in hopes that we will *enter* difficulty with hope. It is that invitation to enter that the gospel sends out. The refusal to accept that invitation is what keeps us from growing old well and open and alive.

In the first sermon in this collection, hope is seen from the other side of betrayal. Others do fail us; we also fail others. Sometimes when others fail us, we participate, by failing to believe in God's hope just because human hope has crumbled. We become part of our own betrayal.

In the second sermon, hope is offered to the elder brother within each of us. That hard working man was in the way of his own hope: his very virtue became an obstacle.

In the third, hope is seen playing its best role; when recession affects the economy, our hope is also bruised. The recession carries at least this silver lining: it requires us to distinguish between God and the economy. Following the comfort of Isaiah, we are encouraged to "walk here . . . this is the way."

In the fourth, we right-size our hope. More often than not what we are hoping for is grandiose, giant—not human size. Matters of scale are important to matters of hope. The burning-bush text shows how holy we are no matter how small we also are.

In the fifth, we see hope as the reason we turn the other cheek—there is surely no other. Hope that lies beyond the hope in violence is assessed, again using the text of the prodigal son.

These sermons were originally preached to the First Congregational Church in Riverhead, New York, during Lent of 1992. At that time nearly one third of the congregation was unemployed or under-employed. The main street of the village had lost another group of its shops. Our church's soup kitchen was feeding 100 people weekly. The high school was in a near race riot. And the line of women and children at the door—wanting diapers, medicines, food, and shelter—was very long. Oddly, in that difficult season, we made friends with our hope. We were by the grace of God able "to turn the Valley of Achor into the door of hope" (Hosea 2:15).

Many of the sermons were also preached at Star Island at the UCC family camp, August 1-8, 1992. There, from an ancient pulpit looking out at the Atlantic Ocean, six miles out from Portsmouth, I found reason to remember that "hope is based on nothing less, than Jesus' blood and righteousness," an odd recollection in so sterling a spot. I remember thinking at the opening of the week that if there were hard times anywhere, surely they were not here. But hope is not something we need just because times are hard. It is also something that pulses within our own blood, perhaps driving even deeper things, like the changes of the tide, the sound of the gull, the dawn and the dusk. In the first sermons here, I speak of a more urban, wintered hope. I discovered its application in summer as well.

The last few sermons have more sunlight than the first few. Hoping for acceptance is something we all do. No matter how many tough guys tell you they "don't care what other people think," don't believe them. There is a little lost sheep in all of us. Hoping for love has an equal universality: the trick is learning to love. Then we can find love.

Being able to hope in the Church is, for me at least, at all seasons exquisitely difficult. Entering that difficulty with hope has proved most fruitful, even if opening the first door into the trouble is the hardest thing I am ever called to do. Being able to hope when death comes to someone too early has the same rhythm: first you enter the difficulty, then you find God.

Standing outside the gates of pain permits too little encounter with it; you have to wade in the water. There you find God and others, wading with you.

The final sermon, "Hope to Get High," takes Pentecost as its partner, and has some fun. It is a dance above the hard times, that place from which hope is usually calling.

The fact that hope is a survivor does not mean that it likes bad things to happen. Hope is not opportunistic. The fact that hope gets the jobless out of bed in the morning does not mean that it is equally happy in economic difficulty. Hope works for justice, works for fairness, and wants people to have jobs and salaries good enough to support their optimism. Hope also has plenty of work to do even in economically excellent times. Hope also has wings; it dances. It flies above the hard times while being engaged in them. As long as you give hope a little time off from its hard working character, you'll be surprised how quickly it can turn even hard times into good ones.

CHAPTER ONE

Then Jesus was led up by the Spirit into the wilderness to be
tempted by the devil. He fasted forty days and forty nights,
and afterwards he was famished. (Matt. 4:1-2)

Weeping may linger for the night,
but joy comes with the morning. (Ps. 30:5b)

# Hope When Others Fail Us

Almost no one faces the end of the twentieth
century with optimism. Even fewer face it with
hope. The alarms may always have been there,
but now they have a megaphone: the ozone;
toxic dumps; nations, decades old, disappear in days;
homelessness; lack of respect; violence in our neighborhoods. We all know the list by heart.

Publicly we look under every rock for a hopeful sign
and find nothing. Privately a similar emptiness prevails.
Children are even more lost than adults—and it is the rare
adult who claims to have a hope to hand on. We see the
children as "realistic." Teenagers are even more so.

Suffering the effects of a recession on top of the preexisting gloom and doom—what some are calling a decession—a lot of people are asking themselves the question of hope. The public problems are beginning to pinch. The question of hope takes this shape: On what do I rely? Do I rely on the economy's running well? Yes, of course. Do I rely on a certain degree of environmental durability? Also of course. But what if the economy doesn't run well, and what if I can't communicate with my teenager? What if the environment does have one of its widely foreseen disasters? What if I can't face my high school yearbook any more? What if my old certainties rust or fade? What if the things on which I rely slip away? What if my old confidence disappears? When I am alone, without crutches or culture, then, on what do I rely?

> *"We may be asked to live in times for which we were not prepared."*

There is nothing wrong with relying on what you relied on in high school. That somehow you would live in good times, that your self-confidence would last, that the water you drink would taste good, that there would be a job for you. It is not a sin to rely on the world. What we are learning is that it is wrong only if that is all we rely on. Some of us may be called to live in more interesting times. We may be asked to live in times for which we were not prepared. We are not the first generation in history to be signed up unwillingly for postgraduate work.

Georgene Johnson, a forty-two-year-old mother of two, intended to run a race. Two races were being run at the same time and place, the 26.2 Cleveland marathon and a 6.2 mile minimarathon. When Georgene bolted from the starting line, she assumed she was running with a small number of mid-distance runners. About four miles later, she realized that she had actually started with 4,000 runners in the long marathon. She had never run more than 8 miles before. Facing all 26 miles was intimidating. According to *The Christian Ministry* Georgene made it and said the next day, "As stupid as I felt out there running, I'm proud of myself. I guess I was in better shape than I thought. I feel fine although my knees are really sore this morning" (March 1992).

> *"Optimism carries us forward until it doesn't carry us anymore; then we need to develop hope."*

Most of us are in a lot better shape than we think we are. Most of us have also signed up for the wrong race. We are following the crowd when we could be following Christ. (There are no shoulds to hope.) Pastors are no exception. As Henri Nouwen put it, "If pastors are uncertain of what is absolutely essential in ministry, they tend to lose themselves in the merely important." We share this problem with humanity. We get pretty good speed up, but we're running in the wrong race. We get stuck in the important when the essential is calling our name. Optimism carries us forward until it doesn't carry us anymore; then we need to develop hope.

Before we can learn the practice of hope, we have to clear the path of judgments. There is nothing inherently wrong with following the crowd. Or running the same race that everybody else is running. Jesus only began his ministry in the wilderness; he did not stay there.

We are part of one another, humans are supposed to live together, not in some independence but in some interdependence. Think of Georgene's embarrassment—with the same tenderness that she applied to herself—at having followed the crowd. So what? I made an interesting mistake. There is no reason to become so judgmental about the crowd. Or about how long we relied on "externals" to carry us through.

Christ is not opposed to the world but is rather a deeper face to the world. If we stick with the old punishments—naughty you for following the world and not Christ—we won't get very far. We'll simply trade one saddle for another.

The difference between optimism and hope is that optimism has humanity as its foundation; hope has God. One is a better soil in which to grow than the other. Following the crowd permits the optimism of society; it does not permit the hope of Jesus.

Some people are still too young to understand the difference between hope and optimism. Life has given them insufficient reasons to mistrust self-reliance. Parents tell their teenagers not to run in a pack, not to be led around by their peers—but the same parents often forget how much fun it is to feel a part of things, to not stand out, to enjoy the crowd's approval. The same people forgot how easy it was for them to be silent when another person was being attacked with gossip. Or how easy it was to turn the other way as the office manager accused a co-worker unfairly. We want to be a part of the crowd—and if 4,000 people take off in a race we weren't prepared for, most of us will probably still sign up.

Once we can become more comfortable with our own optimism and our own crowd, we will be ready to receive the gift of hope. And some of us will be as lucky as Georgene. We will make it to the end with nothing more than sore knees. But life will also toss us opportunities to travel alone. Wilderness has a funny way of showing up in people's lives uninvited. Some will find that the long race of the big crowd weakens us. We will stumble, we will fall, and we will not find any of the other runners stopping to pick us up.

In this way we will join Jesus in the wilderness. We will find ourselves left with only the optimism of our choice. And we will become hungry for hope, hope the size of our days.

> *"Worry seems to have become the national pastime."*

We come to hard times hoping for hope. Hoping for a little stillness, hoping to relearn the trick of quiet, hoping to find a place to rest on our long journey. Some of us have lost hope in our spouses. Some have lost it even in our churches. Worry seems to have become the national pastime. Most of us would be glad to join a race behind some leader, just to feel a part, just to have the consolation of the group. But no leader wants to lead us.

I get a newsletter from the American Society of Boomers. They want me to join, mostly I think to create a countervailing organization to the American Association of Retired Persons, which they swear is taking all the money away from my generation. The check-off list I found quite amusing. I can check "Yes, I want to help." Or I can check that I am not interested. Or the No column, "My house is paid for, my retirement is assured, my kids will get full scholarships." They *encourage* me to worry in the membership application form. Then they want to know my income level and they state all the obvious choices. The last one is "Afraid to look." Finally under the question of my interests, I can check social security or federal income taxes or the environment or child care or deficit spending or national debt or next month's rent or mortgage. How could I not worry when faced with that list, which does fairly accurately describe my lost generation?

> *"Society is important; God is essential."*

Hope is the antidote to worry. It has at least three parts. One is its communal face; another, its individual face; and the third, its divine face. Hope is not just any one of these.

First, hope's communal face. We find hope in and through one another. Once again, it is not alone versus the crowd, not wilderness versus civilization, not even individual versus society. Rather it is that the crowd can only take us so far, that society can carry us only so far, then we must go the rest of the way alone. Society is important; God is essential. Georgene may have been running with the group, but the fuel that kept her going was inside her, not them.

Muriel Spark tells a wonderful story about traveling from South Africa to England during the war.

> We went from Cape Town to Liverpool by way of the Azores. The voyage took three weeks. It was a dangerous journey. But it is curious how a sense of danger diminishes in proportion to the number of people who participate in the risk. On this occasion, as on others during the war, being "in it together" took off the edge of fear.

The crowd can give this comfort, the comfort of being "in it together." Even that silly baby boomer stuff gives that comfort. So what if there won't be any social security left? We will be in it together. That is optimism. Hope differs from the optimism of shared danger. Hope releases days from worry because your heart is so full of God that there is no room in it left for fear.

Hope also understands that the crowd may turn on you and that you may have to turn on the crowd. I was thinking about what I hoped for prior to a church retreat. I realized my hope was too small. I just hoped that we would not quibble, that someone or something negative would not take us over and run us around. That hope is too small. It is a hope that fears the crowd. I realized that I should have hoped that we would have a sense of being in it together. I think you see the difference, not just that the crowdness of us will refrain from being negative but that the crowdness of us will turn positive.

> *"Hope always knows that things will work themselves out. It doesn't always know when."*

It may be a first. According to the Minneapolis *Star Tribune* a priest in San Antonio, Texas, has sought an injunction against a parishioner. At Our Lady of Sorrows Church, one member insisted on singing loudly during the service. The problem was not the volume but the songs. Apparently the woman's selections were not listed in the order of worship. "We don't mind her coming to church," the priest, Alexander Wangler, said. "We just want her to sing the same thing everyone else is" (October 3, 1992).

This anecdote describes the way that our groups can offer us hope and the way too much individuality threatens to kill us. When we are together, we need to sing the same song. That song is the song of Jesus Christ, not the grabby greedy worry of the devil.

But sometimes we will have to sing our own song. Hope will have to put on its individual clothes. The wilderness face of hope is most crucial at the times when we can't or don't join the crowd, when our own different drummer drums. Again, hope is that fullness from God that allows no room for fear in the heart. The heart is preoccupied with hope. So even the fears that come when we have to walk alone don't have a nesting place. Ruben Alvez says that hope is hearing the melody of the future and dancing to it today. Hope always knows that things will work themselves out. It doesn't always know when. But it always imagines the time when the devil will give up and go home and when we will be able to rejoin our community. The individual may have to hope alone. But her hope is that the time is coming when she may hope again with others, and hope again in others.

Finally, hope has a divine face. It is cruciform. It is the shape of Jesus Christ. It is the absolute certainty that the cross is real but not final. Think about what Jesus had to go through. He had to go against the crowd on behalf of the crowd. He had to suffer at the hands of the crowd. And he did not, while facing the crowd, lose faith in the crowd.

Neither on our own, no matter the strength of our faith, nor in our community—that nice word for crowd—will we find enough hope to hang on. We will descend into optimism. And optimism can't carry us. Or we will focus on the merely important and lose track of the essential. What we will need is hope that Jesus Christ still hopes, despite his suffering. And Jesus Christ does still hope.

I think of the cameraman who was on assignment in Azerbadjan. He was there to record the Armenian war for his network. At one point he found a pile of bodies, some scalped, some deep in rigor mortis. He put down his camera and began to cry. He cried uncontrollably and refused to take anymore pictures. His hope here is phenomenal. It is the size of the hope we need for our days. Had he kept filming, it would have been an act of hopelessness. He would not have really been seeing, despite the sophistication of his lens. He would have such a hardness of heart that neither fear nor hope could make a room in it. By his crying we see that he has hope in humanity. Yet that pile of bodies is not us, but only a stop in our wilderness. By crying he declares hope in himself, that even when he sees the inhumanity of humanity, he will not accept it—or permit it. And he demonstrates hope in God—because it is God who will heal his tears. You know how. God will be able to say, "I know. I understand. We're in this together. They did the same thing to my Son. He ran the long race—and you can too. You're already in better shape than you think you are. Don't be afraid of tears. Be afraid only when you can't hope enough to cry anymore."

Weeping may last all night long, but joy will return to you in the morning.

# CHAPTER TWO

> [The elder brother] answered his father, "Listen! For all these years I have been working like a slave for you, and I have never disobeyed your command; yet you have never given me even a young goat so that I might celebrate with my friends." (Luke 15:29)

# Hope for the Elder Brother

A little girl is drawing away madly at a picture. Her teacher comes up and asks her what she is drawing. "I am drawing God."

"Oh, no one knows what God looks like. You can't draw God," the teacher responds.

"They may not know what God looks like now, but they will know when I am done."

That could be a good motto for a church. Very few know what God looks like, but when we are done, they'll know. They'll know what God looks like because they will look at us and get a glimpse of God.

Oddly many people find their hope blocked by churches

rather than aided by them. Lots of people believe more in God than they do in church.

We recently had a retreat for the deacons and trustees of our church. There I got a glimpse of God—of what God looks like, of the treasure in earthen vessels that we are supposed to see in the Church.

Openness, smartness, critical thinking, laughter, acceptance of the incompleteness of one another—each of these aspects of God, we experienced ourselves.

> *"We all have moments when we are sitting in a pigsty of our own making."*

We studied the text of the prodigal son—and tried to locate ourselves in the biblical story. Most of us could identify with the sinners whom Jesus sat at table with. We knew what it felt like to be ignored or not to matter or to be ridiculed and put down by fancier people, like the scribes and Pharisees. We also knew what it was like to be a scribe or Pharisee, to be one who looks down. One who puffs up and then looks down. And we even had a glimpse of what it would be like to be Jesus, one sitting at the table with sinners who got in trouble for it.

Everyone could identify with the story's odd hero, the prodigal. We all have moments when we would like to take the money and run; we all have moments when running away looks like the best solution. And we all have moments like his of being ashamed that we ran away, wondering how we could have been so stupid as to think that we could make it on our own. We all have moments when we are sitting in a pigsty of our own making.

And some could even identify with God as symbolic parent, who as a parent did not know how to reject his son, even though his symbolic son—the prodigal—had rejected him.

> *"What we learn from the story is that elder brothers need to learn how to ask for what they need."*

But the lion's share of identification was left for the elder brother. The one who never did much of anything wrong, who worked away in the field, who took care of the home fires. The Jimmy Stewart character in the Christmas story *It's a Wonderful Life*. Every time you turn around his younger brother is having all the fun. It is the elder brother part of us that interferes with our hope. We can learn from his mistake. .

He didn't ask for what he wanted. He complained about what someone else was getting. He is a classic case of the grumbler who instead of saying "I want my own party" says, "How come he's having one instead of me?" It's very hard to give to the grumbler. But to the one who claims his inheritance it is almost impossible to say no.

The prodigal son claimed his inheritance. The father gave it to him. The elder brother just kept hoeing, thinking somebody else would thank him or give him something. He didn't want to have to ask. What we learn from the story is that elder brothers need to learn how to ask for what they need.

In our retreat the lesson about asking surfaced. What was delightful about the retreat is the way we said what we wanted. It wasn't said with the "nanna boo boos" of the elder brother's whine. How come we don't get more attention and the poor get all the attention from the pastor? How come . . . whine, whine?

Instead we spoke with the authority of our own hopes

for ourselves. This is the kind of congregational authority that has made congregations famous. We want more attention paid to our inner life, our inner cohesion, our attention to and with one another. We need to have more fun here. We need to have more peace here. We need to have less work here. There is beauty in elder brothers asking for things for themselves. Each of these desires could have been stated in a nasty way, a condemning way, a judgmental way—or they could be said with a simplicity, an expectancy, a hopefulness, a legitimacy. I want. Not, *I want!*

The elder brother could learn a few things from our church's leadership. Instead of going to the father and complaining about what he didn't get, he could ask for what he wants. When you're done with his party, I hope we can schedule one for me.

> *"Many of us have been encouraged by an unhealthy religion to become whiners."*

I had a sign on my door that was so insightful that it was stolen. "Thou Shalt Not Whine," it said. Whining doesn't get you anywhere. It only moves you to that cul de sac of the spiritual life where all people want to do is shut you up. Whining says you can't do anything, that you don't think anybody can do anything about anything, that you have no hope, and that you would like to pollute everyone else's environment with your hopelessness.

One of the fundamental principles of the spiritual life is that you reap what you sow; that what goes around comes around; that if you treat others well, they will treat you well; that if you are sour and rotten on the inside, you will also be sour and rotten on the outside. The roots of our lives have a queer resemblance to their branches. This principle of the fundamental connection between inside and outside, body and soul, public and private, religion and politics applies to the elder brother's whine.

He was expressing his genuine self. He had allowed that expression to genuinely become a whine. Many of us have been encouraged by an unhealthy religion to become whiners. To not ask for what we need. Our spirits are wounded by this command to whine instead of to ask. Remember one of the fundamental statements of Jesus, ask and you shall receive, seek and you shall find, knock and the door shall be opened unto you? Instead many of us stand around, shoulders hunched, waiting for someone to thank us or to notice us or to remember that while others are squandering, we are saving.

This dysfunctional spirituality is everywhere in our society. Our spirits have been wounded by it. We were taught, too many of us, to believe in a harsh, angry God who expects us to be perfect. This God uses shame to coerce the child—and it is that shame that has caused us as adults to be whiners.

Shame is probably the most damaging way you can treat another person. You mean you want that? You disgusting thing. In shame, a person wants to disappear, to hide. There is a painful self-consciousness, so painful that you don't want to risk asking for anything because you might be noticed.

Shame differs from guilt in many ways. Guilt is a bad inner feeling deriving from the sense that one has done something wrong. Shame is the deeper more profound inner feeling that stems from feeling that one is bad at the core. The elder son didn't really believe that he deserved a party. He was structured to think that he wasn't good enough for a party. That's why he just kept hoeing and hoeing, to prove that he was good enough.

Shame becomes very difficult to heal. God's love has to

get into this inner core of the person—and that inner core is protected by an absolute army. The army is hard at work, being good, and then whining, complaining. The army at our inner core does not ask for change or for recognition, but whines for it—and whining in such a way that no one wants to give it. This way the inner core protects itself and ratifies its own assumptions: "See, I told you nobody wanted to give me a party."

The shame that is widespread in religious culture—and was there since at least the time of the elder brother—comes from a distorted image of God, which suggests that God really hates us and doesn't think we are good enough or could ever be good enough. We end up with flawed images of ourselves, thinking that we are unworthy and unlovable. Then we combine our distorted God with our distorted self to damage relationships—which are the only things that can heal us. The cycle is vicious—ask the children of anyone who was shamed by their parents.

The healing of wounded and shamed spirits is difficult but not impossible. It has to do with remembering who God really is. It has to do with drawing pictures of the true God, not the mean God. When churches such as ours do things like we did in our retreat—in which no one was shamed because people were saying what they wanted without shaming or whining—we draw the picture of the merciful God, the true God, the one who throws parties for prodigals *and* for elder brothers.

CHAPTER THREE

You hear a Voice behind you whispering,
"This is the way, walk here." (Isaiah 30:21b Moffatt)

# Hope in Times of Recession

*H*ope is not optimism. Hope is not so much certainty that things are going to work out as it is a certainty that, even if they don't, we'll still be okay. You may lose your job, and that would be very bad. But it would not be awful. It would not be terrible. It would be significantly inconvenient but basic parts of you would still be okay.

Hope prevents worry. Hope hasn't time to worry. Rather than being optimism, hope is confidence. Confidence is the working boots of hope. Confidence is what hope wears to work, what hope does daily. Hope is what you find at the back of your closet, something that you had forgotten was there. You find your hope at the bottom of your well when and if bad things happen to you. It becomes the thing that lets you get through what you didn't think you could get through.

Everyone has met a person who has gotten through a terrible thing—the death of a child, the suicide of a friend, the loss of a limb. When those of us to whom these things haven't happened think about them happening to us, we recoil in fear. We don't realize that the people who get through these things are just like us. They just had to dig deeper in their closet, lower the bucket deeper into their well. They had to get over the loss of optimism and the gaining of hope. Then they had to put on the working boots of confidence and every day carry on as though the future was still safe, even though they know it is not.

I think of women who have been raped. The thing they want most is to have their old life back, the time before the rape, when they could be optimistic about their safety. These women are no longer able to live by optimism. Even their confidence is shaken. Thus they put on their hope. And hope allows them to live beyond fear. They hope in the God who does not condone violence in a world that sometimes does condone it. These women will not be able to be optimistic anymore. But they will find healing through hope. God will be behind them walking, whispering, "Walk here, this is the way."

> "Confidence is hope's working shoes."

Those people facing layoffs would do well to take a glance at people who have lost their optimism, people who have been raped or suffered other severities. Even when we lose something as close to us as our personal safety, many manage to still carry on. Most do quite well. They are forced to the place beyond and under optimism, that place where God dwells, whispering that we are safe nevertheless. Even if we lose our jobs, we are safe. Even if we lose our street safety, we are still safe. The whisper is that there is a safer place below the loss of safety. That place goes by many names. One of its names is hope. And confidence is hope's working shoes.

The nugget of hope is confidence, the way it walks beyond danger and loss to stay alive every day.

I was reading a story to my daughter's first-grade class the other day. The story was about a seventy-two-year-old woman who didn't think she could draw, so she hid all her beautiful paintings in a closet. At the end of the story, Katie's teacher asked the children how many of them could draw. And they all raised their hands! When you ask six year olds whether they can draw, they all raise their hands. Whereas if I asked almost any adult mixture how many of them could draw, I daresay a much lower percentage would raise their hands.

Hope is about capacity as well as confidence. It is not just that famous one step in front of the other for which most of life's great sufferers are known. Hope also thinks it can draw. Hope is a matter of confidence about our capacity.

This capacity has taken a real beating lately. If you ask most people how to solve the economic downturn of the moment, they say they don't know. They don't know how to draw a human economy. But every now and then you run into someone who does know how to draw it. I think of the AT&T operators who now answer the phones in some parts of the country with these words, "Thank you for speaking with a real AT&T operator." It's probably the union's idea, of course. Faced with automation, there are quite a few people who would like to keep their jobs. Of course machines could do their jobs just as well. But if machines keep doing everybody's jobs, I wonder what is going to happen to everybody. I like the hope that expresses itself as capacity. Thank you for talking to a live AT&T operator.

Or I think of people in our local Greenmarket, a jobs development program for people who eat in the church's soup kitchen. Economically displaced, they are not spiritually displaced. They have hope that they can grow something, do something, make something, amount to something. Human dignity is a magnificent thing. It is hope in its own capacity, long after everybody else has said that you can be replaced by a machine, long after everybody else has said we don't need you anymore. You have been rendered economically useless. Hope says, oh, no I haven't.

> *"Hope is God's whisper to us. God whispers, 'Keep going. The way you are going is the right way.'"*

I remember visiting Peoria, Illinois, at the invitation of the local council of churches. Most houses there were for sale. The realtors had requested that people put a sign on their house if it was *not* for sale so that the neighborhoods didn't look so daunting. But, there on the main square of town, you could eat any kind of food you could imagine. People cooked their own specialties in the morning and sold them at lunch. The life in the center of town was magnificent—because people wanted to be together and eat together, unemployed or not. I never had a better tasting pirogi than that day in Peoria. People say there wasn't a broken lawnmower in town either, or an unwashed window. Mind you, money wasn't changing hands, but services were. Peoria taught me that you can have a simple economic life and actually enjoy it. I saw the people there doing just that.

In the biography of the life of Gutzon Barglum, the

sculptor who carved the figures of the four U.S. presidents at Mt. Rushmore, South Dakota, the story is told of the woman who swept up the pieces of rock he chipped away from the stone. Amazed, this woman watched the head of Lincoln emerge from the stone. When the work was finished, she simply had to ask, "How did you know Mr. Lincoln was in that stone?" The sculptor obviously couldn't answer that question. None of us can answer the question of how we know we can draw, how we know that we *do* matter.

How *do* we know that there is life despite the stones that have been thrown at us? But alive we are. How do we know that there is life in the stone that is our heart? We don't know how we know. Instead, we know that we find hope when we need it. And hope puts on its working boots and makes us capable of doing what we have to do. And sometimes what we have to do is carve Abraham Lincoln out of great stone. And sometimes we have to get out of bed in the morning and make pirogis and take them to the center of town. And sometimes one is harder than the other. I respect the artist, for sure, but even more I respect the person who faces the unsculpted, unimagined day, putting one foot in front of the other. Survival is an art form itself.

So, hope is confidence and capacity. Hope gets out of bed. Hope draws. Hope speaks. Hope acts. Hope puts one foot in front of the other. Hope is God's whisper to us. God whispers, "Keep going. The way you are going is the right way."

I think of a woman in our church who is the first female head of a large agency. I asked her how her work was going. She said that it was going just fine, as long as she kept one foot on the gas pedal and the other foot on the brake pedal, as long as she knew when to move forward and when to stand still. I thought the humor in her comment was wonderful; she recognized some of the double binds she was in: She had to succeed on behalf of so many others; she had a certain hope lying on her shoulders that she was meant to carry. She dared not drop it.

She reminds me of that cartoonist who was asked how she managed the responsibilities of both work and family. She said it was a cinch as long as you knew how to swim upstream in peanut butter with a pack of alligators chasing you. The alligators' favorite food was peanut butter. Same answer as the paradox of the gas pedal and the brake. Sometimes hope has to go beyond confidence and beyond capacity, to walk when it is no longer confident or capable of walking. Hope listens in, then, on the whisper of God. The humor of God. Keep going. The way you are going is the right way.

God has such good manners. God is not a shouter, not a showboat. Rather a whisper. Walk here. This is the right way. And I'm right behind you. I want to whisper this to everyone who has trouble getting out of bed in the morning, to everyone waiting in fear for a pink slip at work. I want to whisper this to those who have been raped and who can hardly bear to look at certain street corners, even though they have to pass them every day. And I want to whisper this to every mother who is on welfare. Hope is confidence. Hope makes us capable of doing what must be done. And even when hope's confident working boots are all worn out, and its capacities withered or disregarded or mocked, still there is a whisper. A whisper straight from God who is always right behind us. Keep going. This is the way, walk here.

# CHAPTER FOUR

*Moses said to God, "If I come to the Israelites and say to them, 'The God of your ancestors has sent me to you,' and they ask me, 'What is his name?' what shall I say to them?"* *God said to Moses, "I AM WHO I AM." (Exod. 3:13-14)*

# Hope the Right Size

*A*t the New Kete Monastery in Cambridge, New York, an exceptional community of monks has gained international renown for training puppies. They have now published their method in a book called *The Art of Raising a Puppy*. The secret, the monks disclose, to the art of raising a puppy is to "know that a dog is a dog"—to know that a dog is a dog. The book concludes with a puppy test, how you know when a puppy is ready to become a dog, and has a poignant epilogue entitled "A New Way of Seeing." As long as we can see a dog correctly, we can raise it properly. Again, the trick is to see that a dog is a dog.

No one less than Pogo made a similar point when he asked, "Why turn a perfectly good frog into a prince?" Why does everyone want to be something different, or presumably better, than they are?

God faced this question. You heard God's answer. Moses has discovered that God is in a holy place, in a burning bush. God wants Moses to tell the people what he has seen. But Moses asks an amazing question: Who shall I tell the people that you are?

> *"Why turn a perfectly decent God into something you can control, you can label, you can identify, you can put in a box?"*

People say that this is the greatest leap forward in all of Old Testament history. The audacity of Moses asking God God's name. Until this moment, the name of God dared not be spoken. It was not written. If anything at all, it was a breath.

And God could have been Pogo responding, "I AM WHO I AM." Why turn a perfectly decent frog into a prince? Why turn a perfectly decent God into something you can control, you can label, you can identify, you can put in a box? Tell the people, God told Moses, tell the people that I AM sent you.

In Amy Tan's novel the *The Joy Luck Club* a daughter has a mother very much like the Christian God. She is too much like God, too eternal, too mysterious, too holy. She has been forced to leave her home when the Japanese invade and burn it. She is rich. She takes her possessions with her and her twin daughters. Slowly, as she puts it, she lays all her hope beside the road. First her flour and her rice. Then her extra clothing. Then her jewels. She gets a bad infection and dysentery. Finally, with the Japanese in hot pursuit, she leaves behind her twin infant daughters. She hides them. She does not want them to see her die, and she knows that she can't carry on anymore. She leaves all her hope beside the road and attaches the money and jewels that are left to the twins' clothing, with a note in the seams of their dresses about where to take them when the invasion is over.

> "She was just like Jesus Christ. He was the son who had to carry too much hope, the hope of eternal being."

The mother survives. The twins survive. But they never see one another again. The mother searches her whole life for them, but she never finds them. She moves to America and there remarries and has another daughter. The daughter tells the story this way. "I am the daughter who had to carry too much hope." She was just like Jesus Christ. He was the son who had to carry too much hope, the hope of eternal being. I AM sent him to do just that.

The daughter who had to carry too much hope describes herself this way: "Unlike my mother I did not believe I could be anything I wanted to be." The reversal here is very important. God is I AM WHO I AM. Humans say, especially in the face of great expectation, "I won't be what I'm not."

Let the human story detail the divine story as well as the divine story details the human one. Let them color each other in. God is I AM. We are also I AM. But we are not gods. We are ourselves. The girl says to her mother eventually—thank God—I can only be me. I can't be the twins you lost. I can only be me.

We have choices here. We can be oppressed by I AM. And we can think that I AM sent us to be sacrificial lambs or at least desperate and therefore creative. Or, and surely the gospel intends this in all its detail, we can be who we are. Because being who we are respects I AM. Because of the eternal being of I AM, we can be the momentary being of who we are. The trick: letting frogs be frogs, princes be princes, dogs be dogs, people be people, and God be God.

# CHAPTER FIVE

> *The younger son gathered all he had and traveled to a distant country, and there he squandered his property in dissolute living. (Luke 15:13)*

# *Hope Beyond the Hope in Violence*

hile changing the sheets on my eight year old's upper bunk bed, I put my hand into something that was downright gooey. Rubbery. Slimy. There on the far wall of his upper level bunk bed was a wide piece of masking tape, taped to the wall, with several hundred rubber bands attached to it.

I knew we had been having quite a few rubber-band battles at home lately. But I had no idea that we had become an armory, that we were harboring an arsenal. I did know that every day the newspaper came wrapped in a rubber band. But beyond that my level of awareness about rubber bands was as limited as it should be.

When I asked my son about his cache, he told me that he needed the rubber bands "to feel powerful." Weapons, he said, make you powerful. I disagreed, in that futile way that parents disagree with children about matters like this. And I said, no, weapons do not make you powerful. Then I suggested that we list a dozen things that make you powerful. I wasn't going to get anywhere disagreeing with him so I decided to extend his argument. "So, rubber bands make you feel powerful. Let's name eleven more things that can make you feel powerful." Here was his list. Of course he counted it because he is very good at following instructions.

"Well, one is rubber bands. Two is guns. Three is swords. Four is slingshots. Five is uzis. Six is. . . . " I got him to stop there.

"Okay. Okay. How about some other kinds of things? Like maybe words."

"No, Mommy, words do not make you powerful."

"Okay. How about friendship?"

"Okay, friendship. Especially if your friends have weapons."

By then we had way too long a conversation for a forty-four year old and an eight year old so just to please me, he added a few nonviolent items to the list and left. Words, friendship, and having food to trade.

> *"The children have run away from home. They have run away to the land where might makes right."*

My prodigal son has already run away from home— to live in a culture that is foreign to my own values. So, don't worry, has yours. They have all run away from home.

42

For the second time this year a young man associated with my congregation has had a knife brandished at him in the public school system. Another of our recent confirmands reports a cache of weapons in the locker two down from hers. Rubber bands get bigger as they grow up.

The children have run away from home. They have run away to the land where might makes right, the land where fear reigns, the land where telling the truth will only get you in trouble.

And don't think for a minute that I am about to blame the children. The prodigal son ran away for a reason. He was nothing more than what he had been made. Our children are nothing more than what we have made them. In our local school right now the teenagers are acting out the drama of the larger community. We write the script. They act it out.

Weapons, the script says, make you powerful. The bigger your car, the more powerful you are. The bigger your house, the more powerful you are. The louder and ruder you can shout at a town board meeting or a school board meeting, the more powerful you are. The fact that your power achieves little but the need to maintain itself is rarely noticed. The fact that power is a subhuman goal for a child or a parent or a society is rarely noticed. Power is an embarrassing destination for a child, or an adult, or a community.

And yet here we are, far from home, out here in a pigsty, eating pig food. My home town of Riverhead, New York, in its bicentennial year, is not at home with itself. Some people want to blame black people: "They're the reason we're so far from home." Others want to blame white people: "No, it is they who are making a mess of our community." Rubber bands are being popped all over the place. The youth imitate the community's larger squabbles. Only some of them use knives.

What no one wants to do is to go home. At least the prodigal son woke up in his pigsty and said, "Wait a minute. I could be home. I could be eating my father's food." His passage home, his ticket back, was to acknowledge his mistake, his sin in leaving home in the first place. And you know what he found when he got back? He found a father waiting. A father forgiving. A father leaning over the fence, looking, hoping that the son would return. No recrimination. No beltings, no beatings, no weapons, no I told you sos. Instead disarmament, that time when we lay our weapons down so that we can get ready to embrace one another.

> *"The gospel consistently reports self-righteousness as the sin from which there is no return."*

If we are to find hope beyond our hope in violence, we, too, will have to acknowledge the mistakes we have made in running away. We will have to see how filled our hands are with weapons. And we will have to lay our weapons down.

The truth of the whole matter about black people and white people is that both are wrong. Not that one group is wrong and the other is right—not that white is right or black is right—but that both groups are wrong. We are wrong in the way we want to be sure we are right. The gospel consistently reports self-righteousness as the sin from which there is no return. Each of the many sides—for there are surely more than two—wants to be right. No one wants to get back home. Everyone wants to simply be right. You can't get home and also be right. That's what the prodigal learned, and that's what we will also have to learn. If we want hope in hard times, we will have to learn how to admit being wrong. And then to take one more step.

It is not racist to say something negative about a black person. And it is not racist to say something positive about a white person. What may be the most interesting thing about our community is that we are neither perfect nor evil. Instead we are both good and bad. We are each a mixture of good and evil. So are you. And so am I.

Thinking about racism has taken away a lot of our hope. We want so much to be right—so desperately to be right—that we covet it rather than the capacity to hope. If we are to turn the corner toward home, a lot of people are going to have to admit that they have made mistakes. I am a card-carrying racist. I see color where I shouldn't. The turn toward home for me is understanding that I colorize. The turn home for me is understanding that I have privileges as a white person that others don't have because of their color. My Father needs to hear that I know I have sinned before I can get home. The same is true of every person who is ripping off the welfare system. They also have to acknowledge their mistakes to get back home. It is not my job to acknowledge others' mistakes, but rather it is my job as one who hopes for hope to acknowledge my own.

The point is not how wrong everyone has been, how we have all conspired to make a fairly dangerous mess here and in most places American, but rather how urgent is our need to get home.

When we get home, consider what we will see. What might our communities be if we would just get sick enough of eating in the pigsty of self-righteousness and remember that our Father has a banquet spread out before us? Just think.

> ## "When all we hope for is the victory of the violent, we violate the Bible."

I can imagine high school students of all colors refusing to act in the same old play as their parents. I can imagine a meeting in which black teenagers and white teenagers said that they wanted the police out of their school and the disciplinarians out of their school because they wanted to take care of business themselves. The code would be as follows: We will always accuse somebody who threatens with a weapon. We will always testify against them. We will keep one another safe. I can imagine teenagers taking racial matters into their own hands and rather than make a mess of them, realize their own authority to be in charge of themselves.

I can imagine meetings where adults decided that, instead of being rude to one another and claiming their "rights," they would ask one another questions. Instead of offering the pointed finger, offering the outstretched hand. Have you noticed how ugly meetings in some communities can be?

I can imagine a community where the concord and quiet were so deep that no one would even think of holding an athletic practice on a Sunday morning. Don't think I have switched subjects. I have not. One of the reasons that we are in exile, in our pigsty, is that we don't value the right things. If you don't keep first things first, second things will always compete. We value the wrong things. We value the rubber band of being busy, the machine gun of Sunday shopping, the slingshot of the market, and the pistol of privatized life. We prefer the armor of "not liking politics," as though we had a choice. Politics is the air we breathe. You want more biblical sermons? We'll give you more biblical sermons. But don't ever think that the Bible is immune to politics.

When all we hope for is the victory of the violent, we violate the Bible. When we violate the Bible, we lose many of the chances we might have had for hope.

The prodigal son thought that if he left home he'd find a better way to live. He did not. Like the prodigal, many of us have left home on the matter of race. America has left home, and what we have found is that the food outside of the house of the Lord doesn't taste nearly as good as it does inside.

> *"No race has a corner on the pigsty; we all seem to be paying our rent to its tenement."*

But remember the gates. You just don't get to go back inside. God will welcome you when you get there, but not until you have been through the fire of forgiveness, not until you can say that you did something wrong. I just once would like someone to start a sentence by saying, "I am a racist and. . . . " What we keep hearing around here is, "I am not a racist but. . . . " The correct formulation is *I am . . . and*, not *I'm not . . . but*. Prodigal language. Prodigal speech. Most white people are racists. I'll tell you a little secret. Most black people are also racists. They have internalized the message that the point of life is to be better than someone else, to be right, to be powerful. Being better than others, being right and being powerful, is to choose to live in a pigsty. It is living outside of home. No race has a corner on the pigsty; we all seem to be paying our rent to its tenement.

Conversely the ability to be wrong, the ability to be weak, the ability to share power in a community, these are the marks of a home. They are the prelude to hope. Remember home, that place where when you have to go there they have to take you in?

Imagine what it looks like for God. Standing at the gate. Leaning to look down the road. Wondering if we will ever come back. Hoping all the good food won't go to waste. Ready to throw us a big party if we would just turn the corner toward home. Home is where the hope is.

# CHAPTER SIX

> "Which of you, having a hundred sheep and losing one of them, does not leave the ninety-nine in the wilderness and go after the one that is lost until he finds it?" (Luke 15:4)

# Hope for Acceptance

I f cats didn't run away from time to time—to join the circus or whatever it is that they do—those of us who love cats might never realize how much we love them. Because they do run away from time to time, children and adults get a practice run on grief. We get to try out for the olympics of loss, the world series of grief.

This is what happened with Rocky. Rocky Raccoon slipped into the room on my birthday two years ago. He was tortoise shell striped and stuck in the nursing mode. He nursed people's blankets. Because of this addiction, one of the kids could usually get him in bed. He was my son's present to me, but my daughter's blanket had more fur, so she hoarded the cat.

For days after Rocky slipped away—to the circus or backpacking across Europe or whatever—Katie could be found crying little tears. Jacob got his entire first grade to put up signs, Lost Cat, replete with pictures. Isaac was more stoic. Probably too old at eight years, eleven months, to really grieve. He knew too much already at that age of what it really means when something is gone and may never, ever come back.

Most of us do by his age. When we say, "I lost it!" we know what we mean. That phrase *I lost it* can be heard more and more. We hear it in Rod Stewart's music, I had a job, I had a girl, I had, I had, I had. Then that careening chorus, "it seems like I'm riding on the downtown train."

Or you will hear people describe a phone conversation in which someone insults them. Their response is so very descriptive that only slang can truly describe. "I lost it! I just lost it!"

They are telling you that they were returning insult for insult, that any sense of courtesy or propriety had joined the circus or was backpacking across Europe. "When she said that, I just lost it!"

> *"All of us who 'lost it' on the phone or elsewhere this week are no doubt looking for a way to find it."*

The text of Luke 15:1-10 is all about loss. It is about some striking assumptions that Jesus makes about what people do about loss. He thinks that we go off looking for what we have lost. A shepherd has one hundred sheep. One is lost. He tells the gathered crowd that of course the shepherd takes off in search of the lost one. You have ten coins. One is lost. Of course, Jesus says, if you lose one piece of silver, you take off to find it.

Certainly we did look for our cat. And many people in Rod Stewart's generation are looking for a job or a girl or both. All of us who "lost it" on the phone or elsewhere this week are no doubt looking for a way to find it. To apologize or at least not to lose it again. Temper is a very bad thing to lose. Because even when you find it again, it may be too late.

I agree that we would look for a lost coin. It is this missing sheep that I am not sure many of us would go for. We still have ninety-nine. What I want to do here is to use that one lost sheep as a way into the matter of loss and grief.

There is more than one way to approach the subject. Most of us are familiar with the stages of grief: that first stage of anger, why did the sheep run away in the first place; the second stage of bargaining, if God will just bring the sheep back, we promise not to ever yell at it again; the third stage of depression and disengagement, where we are sad, isolated, untying knots, staying at home nights; and the final stage of acceptance, where we learn to live without the sheep.

This healthy pattern of grief applies to things that are not only lost for the moment but lost for good. The loss of a spouse to cancer, a divorce in a truly broken marriage, the wedding ring we happened to leave on the sink at camp. When we have really lost something, when something is really gone, we have to go through a process.

> *"Hope for acceptance works on both a death scale and a life scale."*

Typically, but not always, we get angry. We bargain. We get depressed. And finally we accept our loss. We go on.

This healthy pattern of grief, which does lead to acceptance, is not what Jesus is talking about here. He is talking about finding what is lost—not about accepting the loss of what is lost.

We have to be careful not to confuse the two. Hope for acceptance works on both a death scale and a life scale. Here Jesus is talking about the life scale. The sheep is lost; find it. The coin is lost; find it. Jesus is describing that behavior of God toward us which is understood as unconditional acceptance. We can't even run away from God. We can try. But we can't do it because God will keep trying to find us.

On the death scale, in human circumstances, accepting loss is fine. On the life scale something different is true: we may continue to hope to find or to be found. We may continue to hope for positive acceptance of God's gifts, not just negative acceptance of what we have lost. We may be one of a hundred sheep, but that one hundredth sheep is as important to God as the other ninety-nine. God is out there looking for us, offering us unconditional acceptance. The trick for us is accepting that acceptance.

We must accept that acceptance, accept that gift, and do so graciously. If loss operates on a death scale, in stages, surely accepting our acceptance does as well.

I think of the great American transcendentalist and philosopher Margaret Fuller saying, "I accept the universe." Thomas Carlyle, another New England sage of the same period, said in response to her pronouncement, "By God! she'd better." As we move toward positive acceptance, surely this is the first stage. It is to realize that we don't have that many choices not to. At the bottom of the religious barrel, on both the life scale and the death scale, there is this matter of our acceptance of the universe. Do we accept it only in part and grudgingly or heartily and altogether? Shall our protests against certain things in it be radical and unforgiving, or shall we think that, even with evil, there are ways of living that must lead to God? If we accept the whole, shall we do so as if stunned into submission, as Carlyle would have us—By God! we'd better—or shall we accept the universe with enthusiastic assent?

William James argued that morality may accept the universe as a yoke and may obey it with the heaviest and coldest heart. But in religion, James said, in its strong and fully developed manifestations, the service of the highest is never felt as a yoke. Dull submission is left far behind and a mood of welcome, which may fill any place on the scale between cheerful serenity and enthusiastic gladness, has taken its place.

A mood of welcome of the universe is surely the second stage, beyond acceptance—acceptance first, then welcome.

William James said it best in his *Varieties of Religious Experience*, "It makes a tremendous emotional and practical difference to one whether one accepts the universe in the drab discolored way of stoic resignation to necessity or with the passionate happiness of Christian saints" (p. 49).

James accuses the stoics of passive acceptance of the universe. He talks about the Emperor Marcus Aurelius having a frosty chill about his words "If Gods care for me or for my children, there is a reason for it." Then hear Job cry: "Though he slay me, yet will I trust in him" (13:15 KJV). I love James's metaphors for the difference between Christian and stoic acceptance. Christian is tropical, he says, stoic is arctic. One is hot and enthusiastic, the other is cool and calculating.

"I accept the universe," says Margaret Fuller. By God! she better. Fuller is speaking on that cusp between acceptance and welcome.

For us, the practical applications are many. The first I think would be to deeply understand this matter of stages. Almost the whole culture now knows the Kübler-Ross stages of grief: anger, bargaining, depression, and acceptance. We should learn the stages of positive acceptance, from simple acceptance of our acceptance to positive welcoming of God in our lives. God accepts us, no matter what. We are like a lost sheep to God—and God means to find us. Period. The end. There are no hiding places from God. You may feel lost. You may be lost. But God can and will find you.

> *"There are not good sheep and bad sheep in the eyes of God."*

We are accepted unconditionally. There are not good sheep and bad sheep in the eyes of God. God accepts us without conditions. Therefore we can accept God. We can hope for acceptance from God. We can hope to be accepted by God. And then I think the moral stage that William James talks about kicks in. We then accept the universe, not as something we have lost, as in "I lost it," but rather as something we have found. We have found the joy of accepting the universe—the hot passionate enthusiasm of accepting the universe. Not the "GOD, she'd better," but the "God, I do" kind of acceptance. A consent that is genuine.

Most people spend all their lives complaining about how the universe doesn't accept them. As with so many things, as soon as we reverse that problem, it becomes solvable. Accept the universe, and it will accept you. Deny it, and it will deny you. You want love? Learn to love. Don't wait for someone to love you. You want acceptance? Learn to accept. Don't be passive in your desire for acceptance; be active in your desire for acceptance.

This level of acceptance allows us to carry on with lost cats, lost jobs, lost girls, and lost tempers. It also allows us a level of hope that is deeper than hope itself. It is not hope that things turn out well so much as it is hope that we will accept and enjoy the way things turn out. Religious hope is on a different plane than moral hope.

A bishop in The United Methodist Church said that every year every church deserves a new pastor. And every year every pastor deserves a new church. And that doesn't necessarily imply a pastoral change. A very interesting hope, I think. It is a hope that we can be new, that we can accept one another without conditions, that even though we have been lost to one another, we can find one another. What a beautiful hope, a hope based in the hope for acceptance.

A pastor called me from Tennessee recently to say that the new year had gotten off to a bad start. "My custodian is exposing himself to the Sunday school teachers as they come in to clean up their rooms. My choir director has refused to use the music I requested for reunion Sunday because he says it stinks. My secretary is a tornado, she hasn't found anything in years and now she has lost this Sunday's bulletin. Now, mind you, she would walk off a cliff for you, if she could find the cliff. . . . " She went on long enough to convince me that my problems are really quite small. This pastor has lost it. She surely has to accept some of her loss and then she has to not accept other parts of it. She has to accept the universe, that universe in which we all live where what she is experiencing is unfortunately fairly common. This week in our homes and in our jobs things are not going to be what they should or could be. But we will accept them anyway. We'll change what we can and accept what we can't and beg to know the difference between the two. We won't find every missing cat or even every missing sheep but we won't walk around lost either. Once we were lost, but now we're found. Once we were blind, but now we see. We see that God has accepted us. And we accept God.

# CHAPTER SEVEN

> *I have fought the good fight, I have finished the race, I have kept the faith. From now on there is reserved for me the crown of righteousness. . . . At my first defense no one came to my support, but all deserted me. May it not be counted against them! But the Lord stood by me and gave me strength. (2 Tim. 4:7-8, 16-17)*

# Hope for Love

Paul is reviewing his life in 2 Timothy 4. He is in jail. He is at the end. He is in trouble. He is pretty much alone. There is very little evidence that the things he loved returned his love, and so he must turn to his inner resources. He removes his gaze from his apparent outside failures. He looks inside, and there he finds the love of Christ. There he finds his hope for a crown alive.

Two things strike me about this passage immediately. One is that Paul is actually not alone at all. He is writing this letter to his good friends. Anyone who has ever shared their trouble with another finds that the very act eases the trouble. As soon as we trust someone enough to say, "I am so lonely," we are not lonely anymore. The speaking has changed the condition. So Paul may feel caught in a fight to defend his life's work. He may feel it necessary to defend himself by saying I have fought the good fight, but he is actually less alone than he thinks he is.

Second, he has not lost his faith. Most people who have failed in love or by love lose their faith when they lose their love. They don't lose it permanently, but rather just for that time when they feel alone. Paul's gaze at his own aloneness leads him to God. First he is led to his friends, to speak about how alone he is. Then he is led to God, to affirm God despite his loneliness.

> *"There is a thing called our 'best,' and it is rarely equal to our hope."*

No one really knows what went wrong for Paul at the end. Many of the apostles were in jail or imprisoned. Several had already been crucified. Many churches had been started. Many people had converted. But clearly Paul had hoped for more, and in the end all he could say was that he had done his best. He is here confessing that he did not do all that he wanted to do but rather that he did his best.

It is worth paying attention to how Paul achieved his confidence that he had done his best. The process is worth imitating. He shared his pain with a friend. He found God in the friendship and in the pain. And then, based in the recognition and speaking about loneliness, he sees that there is a difference between what we hope to accomplish in our lives and what we finally offer. There is a thing called our "best" and it is rarely equal to our hope.

If you spend enough time around older people, you find that many of them are involved in this process of life review. They live a rich inner life, calculating, comparing, musing, remembering. The number of sentences that start with, "I had thought that such and such would be such an important decision and instead it was so and so." In the process of life review we remove the outer envelope and get to the inner core. We get to the message. We get to what our life really wanted to say to us.

Paul goes through this process of opening up his life and looking at it. Most of us do—and you don't have to be near the end to get involved with life review. Søren Kierkegaard actually thought that reviewing your life was a mistake. He compared it to the process of stopping an arrow in flight: as soon as the arrow ceased its flight, it would fall. I couldn't disagree with him more. To rob the action of our life from reflection upon it is to be only half alive. It is only to be soaring and not to be aware that we are soaring. If the great religions of the world agree on anything, it is that the point of our life is to wake up, to be alert, to pay attention, to keep looking for the inner message and not to get distracted by the envelopes.

I remember one of my aunts falling in love with that great expression: you can't tell a pot from its cover. Every time I had a boyfriend, she would say, "You can't tell a pot from its cover." Likewise you can't tell a life from its flight path. The life has to look around and see what the meaning of it was. That process finally has to happen to us alone, as it did to Paul, as it does to most people. We can only hope that when we take a good look at ourselves, we are as pleased as Paul was. We can only hope to see "our best," to be able to tell our friends and our God that we think we fought the best fight we could.

One of the things that is wrong with this life review process and difficult about what Paul is saying is that we don't actually live alone. Or very few of us do. Our life is not just reviewed in a vacuum but actually in a web of love. Families, friends, spouses, children, bosses, doctors, lawyers, chance acquaintances—we are connected. We don't always control every aspect even of our own best. Paul was also connected. It is with great sadness that he reports to Timothy that he has been abandoned by everyone. Surely he loved those people who abandoned him as much as any of us loves any of the people surrounding us. This matter of love—this connection of our life with other lives—becomes the greatest obstacle to review. We may feel that we have done our best but we may not be able to feel that others have also done their best. As long as the arrow is on that flight path—of what we might call unrequited love—the peace that Paul finds here will elude us.

I want to suggest a strategy for arriving at Paul's peace, despite the arrows that have been slung toward ours. The process of life review requires examination of our love more than it does of the way others have loved us. That is the strategy Paul uses so well. The issue is whether we have stayed our course and stayed in love with the things we were committed to—not whether others have. In that great short novel *Death in Venice,* the hero Auschenbach finally says it right when he says, "It is the lover and not the beloved that is having all the fun."

> *"To hope for love is to hope to be able to love, and to be able to love long after others have stopped loving you."*

Love without this kind of personal accountability is not love at all. It is that soft thing that greeting card companies thrive on. It is not genuine love. There comes a time when you have to decide whether the love that puts wrinkles in your life is genuine or not. And there really is only this one test. Not whether you have been adequately loved but whether you have learned to love well. The golden rule is the highest common sense. You can never know what's going on inside someone else's envelope. You can only know what's going on inside your own heart. Do you really love your commitments, your friends, your family? If the answer is yes, you won't have trouble finishing your personal report card with an acknowledgment of having done your best. If the answer is no, the personal report card won't look so good.

To hope for love is to hope to be able to love, and to be able to love long after others have stopped loving you. Paul joins the great poets in acknowledging the golden rule. Again you will hear in their words the summing up pattern of a life review. George Bernanos tells us that "to be able to find joy in another's joy: that is the secret of happiness." Not so much to find our joy but actually to be able to find another's joy. Albert Schweitzer noted that "when people have light in themselves, it will shine out from them. Then we get to know each other as we walk together in the darkness, without needing to pass our hands over each other's faces, or to intrude into each other's hearts." Love protects us from one another as well as bringing us close. Rainer Maria Rilke defined love as when "two solitudes protect and touch and greet each other." Do you see that in Paul's letter to Timothy? He doesn't beg Timothy to take care of his grief. He rather offers him the secrets of his solitude.

The famous writer Brenda Uleland, in a passage from "The Fine Art of Listening," *UTNE Reader,* November/December 1992, says that "if you are a listener, everybody around you becomes lively and interesting." Again we see the golden rule turned from an ethical injunction into a way to help ourselves stay the course.

Sometimes people cannot listen because they think that unless they are talking, they are socially inadequate. There are those people with an old fashioned ballroom training who insist there must be unceasing vivacity and gyrations of talk. But this is really a strain on others. Letting people in, really letting them tell us their stories, will keep love alive in us. Uleland concludes, "You know, I have come to think listening is love, that's what it really is."

One of the turnabouts she makes in this essay on listening is that she says you shouldn't listen to children in the same way you listen to adults. With an adult, you make space in your heart for their story. And then do nothing but receive it. And that's how you know your love is staying alive. You use it to receive another's story by just staying quiet and calm and listening. But with children she talks about the opposite. She says you can trust children with your story. Don't ask them those awful open-ended questions—how was your day, do you like school— because that means you are asking them to entertain you. Instead, every time you see a child, tell him or her something that has just interested you. Meet their bus with the words, "Today I saw a monarch butterfly," or "Today I had grilled cheese for lunch." Listening, she argues, is not passive with children: it is the active encouragement of them to tell their stories. They learn by our modeling. Finally, she says, they should beg us to stop talking so that they can go to sleep rather than us begging them to stop talking so we can!

The art of listening is one way to end up full at the end of a life. It turns the life review into an act of love itself because we have been able to hold on to our ability to love. One more author says it better than any preacher can. From Stendahl, "Love is a well from which we can drink only as much as we have put in. The stars that are shining from it are only our own eyes looking in." Again the golden rule honors us by allowing us to be able to end our lives by saying we did our best to abide by it.

> *"It is Christ's love that takes over when ours dries up."*

For those of us who feel that things are a little out of control these days, a little unraveled, that there is a little less security coming from our banks and our politicians than we might have hoped, Paul's experience of the good fight is very important. It doesn't matter whether we end up in success or failure, in the pink or out of it. It doesn't even matter how well others love us. What matters is whether we remain able to love them, to listen to their stories and to treat them with the respect we treat our own. Then we will be able to say we have done our best.

Of course we dare not let our capacity to love become our only hope for love. It is Christ's love that takes over when ours dries up. And dry up it may. There are "hits," as the football player would say, that we may have to take. It is not easy to keep love alive over the long haul of a life. It is much easier to take the first dozen hits than the second dozen. Many shut down. Many refuse to open themselves to others' stories. They have lost hope for their best. After a while, some just hope to make it through the day, rather than doing their best.

There is no doubt that love contains its own disappointments. As Paul acknowledges so beautifully, they have all left me now. But he still hopes for love! We must still listen to another even when we no longer have much to say! To hope for love in the end is turning out to be much easier than I ever thought it would be. We can actually control quite a bit of the outcome. To do our best is to remain able to love. When we open the envelope of our life, we find our crown, we find ourselves in the company of Jesus. We find our own little victory over death. We fight the good fight and live to tell ourselves the story. Or maybe even to tell our children the story!

# CHAPTER EIGHT

*"If you have not been faithful with what belongs to another, who will give you what is your own? No slave can serve two masters; for a slave will either hate the one and love the other, or be devoted to the one and despise the other. You cannot serve God and wealth." (Luke 16:12-13)*

# Hope for Happiness

Most nineteenth-century cookbooks, especially in North America, contained a joke recipe, something that if you made it was sure to turn out very badly. Maybe too much spice or salt or vinegar. An inexperienced cook would follow the directions and get in terrible trouble; an experienced cook would predict the trouble and not follow all the instructions.

The ladies of Des Moines Iowa produced one book in 1903, in aid of their Missionary Sewing School, and said that they got this recipe from a similar group in Baltimore.

The title is "Cooking a Husband So He Is Tender and Good." The recipe begins by declaring that "a good many husbands are utterly spoiled by mismanagement." It continues with this advice.

Make a clear, steady fire. Set him as near to it as seems to agree with him. If he sputters and fizzes do not be anxious; some husbands do this until they are quite done. Add a little sugar in the form of what confectioners call kisses, but no vinegar or pepper on any account. A little spice improves them but this must be used with judgement. Do not stick any sharp instruments into him to see if he is becoming tender. Stir him gently; watch the while, lest he lie too flat and close to the kettle, and so becomes useless. You cannot fail to know when he is done. If thus treated you will find him very digestible, agreeing nicely with you and the children, and he will keep as long as you want, unless you become careless and set him in too cold a place.

Balance. Proportion. Getting the right ingredients in the right order. These are problems for cooks, problems for wives, problems for husbands, and certainly problems for Christians. How to get it right? How not to overcook or undercook.

> *"Worry about how things are adding up with God, not how things are adding up with Mammon."*

In Luke 16:1-13 we are given one recipe for getting it right. It is actually a recipe for happiness, not nearly as absurd as the one from Baltimore by way of Des Moines but having some of its good sense. The story tells us that you cannot worship both God and Mammon. You must worship God only, and then Mammon will come out right for you.

The steward (manager) tried to do it backwards. He got his ingredients wrong, and it was no joke. What Jesus tells us is that paying and repaying, counting and recounting, adding and subtracting, the whole piddling process of measuring out our life in Mammon's terms, is useless. It can't bring happiness. It won't "get it right." What will make the final ledgers come out right is worshiping God. Then Mammon will fall into place.

Balance. Proportion. Getting the right ingredients in the right order. You cannot worship God and Mammon. Therefore, worship God. Manage Mammon. Worship God. Worry about how things are adding up with God, not how things are adding up with Mammon. Then, we are promised, we will be happy. Maybe we are not promised in so many words, but when Jesus introduces the word *worship* to what otherwise might be an ethical code, we know that he is talking about joy. Let your joy be with God, your bills with Mammon. Don't seek your joy with Mammon. Seek your joy with God. Then, and only then, will you see your bills in their right perspective. When you see your bills in their right perspective, not as primary but as secondary matters, then and only then will you be able to be happy. You cannot worship both God and Mammon, because you will hate the one and love the other. You cannot do both.

What joy and freedom there is in that instruction! It is a recipe for happiness. Worship, therefore, only God. Mammon's business will take care of itself once you get the ingredients in the proper order.

No less a sage than William James said exactly the same thing. He said that it is religion that allows us to be happy. He says that religion, this putting of God first in our lives, is what constitutes liberation from oppressive moods. Religion is the higher happiness, which keeps the lower happiness in check. See the distinction? It is not that Mammon does not yield happiness, but rather that its happiness, if not unchecked by higher happiness, becomes something idolatrous. And soon it becomes something unhappy. Mammon cannot bear the freight of our joy, much less our sorrow. God can bear the freight of both our joy and our sorrow.

James explains this idea by describing a famous picture. It is a painting by the Italian Guido Reni and in it the saint Michael has his foot on Satan's neck. The richness of the picture, he says, is in large part due to the fiend's figure being there. The allegorical meaning is also due to his being there—that is, the world is all the richer for having a devil in it, as long as we keep our foot on his neck.

You cannot worship God and Mammon. But you can enjoy Mammon, even its devilish parts, as long as you keep your foot on his neck. Keep that part of your life in check so that the worship of God may flourish in you.

> *"Happiness is a consequence, not a goal of life."*

This is really not so much spiritual advice as practical advice. It is a way to be happy. It is not just the devil that needs to be kept in check. It is also pleasures. James talks about how wine and food and ecstasy are frequently part of the religious actor's life. We also cannot worship pleasure if we are to be happy. Both pleasure and pain direct our attention to God. If they direct our attention to Mammon, we will soon lose our ability to enjoy them.

I think of what John Updike said about New York. He lives north of Boston, and he describes coming south to my home territory as travel to the place where money matters too much. What a good description of Mammon, that place where money matters too much. When Jesus says you cannot worship both God and Mammon, he is not saying that Mammon is unimportant. Or even that money is the root of all evil. The worship of money is the root of all evil.

It is when we live too long in that place where money matters too much that our happiness gets destroyed.

Updike also says that happiness is best seen out of the corner of our eye. I like this notion that happiness is a consequence, not a goal of life. It also fits with the message of the text. We are not to worship God to get happiness for ourselves. Because that would be worshiping happiness. That would be a tricky, sneaky approach to Mammon. We are to worship God. When God is first in our lives, we will find ourselves happy. We will find Mammon and its receipts lined up in proper form. And we will find ourselves enjoying life. We will appreciate, Updike says, the walk back from the mailbox. We will have the recipes right.

Another cook I read about was the author of a *Newsday* article on apple pie. She titled her article "The Zen of Apple Pie." In the piece she makes the audacious claim that it is not what you put into the pie so much as what you leave out. She puts in no cinnamon, no nutmeg. She insists that the pie is better pure. You cannot worship both God and Mammon, so take God pure. It is at least another approach to the problem of getting the ingredients right.

> *"Precisely when earth has become too much for us, we need to know the way to our home in God."*

Now I want to answer a few arguments that are sure to come if I stop this chapter right now. "How," someone will ask, "can you be happy in a world like this?" Our church secretary told me a terrible story about some people in her family in Florida. They had a home that was badly damaged south of Miami. They also had a time-share on the island of Kauai in Hawaii that was also hit by a hurricane. You can imagine that these people feel that their number has come up. Many of us go through periods in our lives when we feel just this unlucky. How will worshiping God instead of Mammon help us when we are, in the true sense of the word, unfortunate? I'd have to say that it is precisely in such moments that the taking of Mammon too seriously will spoil the broth. Precisely when earth has become too much for us, we need to know the way to our home in God. You cannot serve both God and Mammon. One of the reasons is that Mammon will always blow away. God will survive every hurricane.

Or someone will say that there is too much injustice in the world to ever be happy. I point you to the South African musical *Seraphina*, now a movie. See it if you haven't. The writer of the musical, which has been on Broadway for about ten years, presents a problem for the fourteen-year-old girl Seraphina. Should she participate in the violence of her peers, the necklacing of soldiers? Necklacing is the putting of a tire around the head of a man and lighting it to show that the black South Africans won't take their oppression anymore. I have taught enough South Africans to know that their oppression—by Mammon, not by God, but by Mammon—is utterly horrible. I doubt that there is one of us, were we black and South African, who would not be tempted to violent revolution. In the musical, Seraphina joins in the violence. In the movie, rewritten by the director, she decides against the violence, on the grounds that it will hurt her more than help her. This is, first of all, a pro-God choice, an anti-Mammon choice. I can't wait to see the movie to see how she makes the choice. But it is the words of the director and writer that stick to me today. "People get South Africa all wrong. All they can see is hunger and suffering and pain. What they can't see is that we are very happy people.

When I go home to the fire and to the dance, when I go home to my people, I am happy there. Many of us are happy there. We know, deep in our hearts, that God is with us."

It is to this kind of happiness that God actually calls us. I call it the in-spite-of-it-all kind of happiness. It is the refusal to worship Mammon, to believe that what Mammon says is true; it is the choice to live in God's world, in God's way, even if you cannot always see it visibly on earth. Or in your time-share. My experience with the truly poor has shown Seraphina's message to always be true, as many poor people know how to be happy, in spite of it all. Maybe it is because they don't really have that much choice to worship Mammon, because Mammon hasn't done enough for them to tempt them. I don't know. What I know is that you cannot worship God and Mammon.

Finally I point you to my new best friend, Jane Eyre. You may not remember her or her story, but I do. I have been reading her story all summer, savoring every line. And I have been listening to it simultaneously on my car tape-player. It gets richer the deeper I go into it. There is an uncanny tendency in literature to have female characters suffer. Anna Karenina gets run over by a train. Emma Bovary dwindles. Scarlet O'Hara loses her man. Hester Prynne gets her letter. There has to be a conflict, and it seems that there has to be a loser. Women step over social bounds; they lose their man; then they lose their lives. Jane is different. Jane gets her man. She keeps her life. Early in the book, she says, "I have found out how to be happy in my own way." Now, mind you, Jane is a penniless orphan who falls in love with a man already married to a lunatic. Not exactly a recipe for happiness. But, "I have learned to be happy in my own way." She learned not to depend on Mammon, not to even need her man. She learned to worship God, and found out how to be happy in her own way.

Had Anna Karenina or Hester Prynne or any of the other tragic heroines learned how not to worship Mammon or man, I can imagine different endings to their stories.

You cannot worship both God and Mammon. You need to keep one in one pot and the other in the other pot. That is good, practical news. That is a recipe for happiness.

# CHAPTER NINE

> *We have this treasure in earthen vessels, to show that the transcendent power belongs to God and not to us.*
> *(2 Cor. 4:7 RSV)*

# Hope for the Church

Lawyers say that if you have the law but not the facts in a case, pound the law. And if you have the facts but not the law, pound away at the facts. And if you have neither facts nor law, pound away at the table. Now we know why lawyers do better than most of us: they have a strategy for what to do when the cup turns up empty.

Right behind this advice to fake it is the other lawyerly notion that power is 90 percent illusion. Look like you have it, and everyone will think you do. You only need to have collateral for 10 percent of the power at any given time.

Both pieces of advice contain a great deal of cynicism. They say *sub rosa* that you can fake it—and everyone knows that is not true. What may be an effective technique in the courtroom is not good advice about how to live your life. You can't fake the important things. You may be able to pound the table hard enough to win a case or two. You may wear an expensive enough suit often enough to make people think you have power. They haven't seen your credit card, only your suit. But all the people all the time won't be convinced. And more important, you yourself won't be convinced. You can wear the suit and carry yourself with the walk of the kind of man or woman who would wear such a fancy suit, but inside you'll know who and what you are. Inner conviction does not necessarily follow outer appearance.

> *"You may leave church meetings late at night and stare at a steeple that seems to point down and not up."*

A lot of us are able to look like we love the church. We walk its walk and talk its talk. Our doubts are kept for the interstices and the midnights and the miles we have to walk alone.

If you are like me at all, you both love and hate the church. You hate the way it turns the magnificent into the mundane and does so with astonishing regularity. You hate the way the minority of table pounders wind up with power over the majority who have a few facts and a lot of gospel. You despise the institution's unwillingness to confront the phonies and instead to tolerate them in the name of something unbiblical like "being nice." And you fear that there never really was a church like the one Jesus recommended—that the church has always been a weak instrument for justice and that from the beginning the institution has maimed the faithful, allowing control to manage freedom.

You leave church meetings late at night and stare at a

steeple that seems to point down and not up. You wonder how so many people could be so stupid. Then you find yourself back there in the morning, hugging the one other person who thought the meeting equally insane and vowing to stick with him or her until the steeple rights its direction, or you hum an old hymn and find yourself crying. You find church in the same interstices where you found the doubt.

People who love the church as much as they hate it have a major spiritual problem—a popular spiritual problem but a major one nonetheless. We are bumpy where we should be seamed. We are unconnected at precisely the place where we should be connected.

> *"Can the search for God become an integrity, even if you have to look through the rubble of the institutional church on the way?"*

*Religion* comes from *religare,* to bind. When the seams of religion fray, we come up with the popular religious problem. The problem's name is integrity. We outsiders have it and church insiders have it. If I both love and hate the church as much as I seem to, what am I doing giving my life or my highest allegiance to it? Don't I commit the lawyerly sin of faking it? And don't people see my tatters? Don't they see how weak my faith in God really is?

Or is there something in the very return, in the coming back after disappointment, in the constant testing of the very seams, that shows strengths? Can the search for God become an integrity, even if you have to look through the rubble of the institutional church on the way?

Obviously, I think yes. Or think enough yes that I am

willing to continue the search for God "inside" the church. (Don't worry. I look outside also.) My desperation for inward connection is serious enough that I can't stop looking inside the church for God. I was too attached to the church as promise as a child to give up on it. The grief would be so much more than just the loss of my adolescent innocence about how things are supposed to be. It would also mean the end of very large parts of me. I need hope the way I need food. And I need to hang on to at least some of the hope of my youth!

The church is an exercise in inner fitness, in finding the place where the seams come together. Life in the church is exactly what the scripture says: It is treasure encased in earthen vessels. Life in the church is a treasure hunt for the integrity of the inner and the outer. In these latter days of church decline and church fear yelling above church grace, our inner, hungry hope is much larger than our outer experience.

We too often go to church hungry and leave hungry. If I were to describe our current stage of spiritual fitness, I think I would use the word *cleft*. Cleft, as in "rock of ages, cleft for me. Let me hide myself in thee." We have fallen out of grace. We are desperate for a place to hide and to rest and to hold on to whatever integrity we can patch together. But God keeps pushing us out of our cleft into the church, the world, the uncleft places. And so we fall in and out of grace—and are caught at each new level of difficulty by a new cleftedness! The interstices are both trouble and promise, like the woman who greets you the next morning and says, "You know I had the same awful experience you had at that meeting last night. What shall we do about it?" She becomes our church, the place where we can rest before the next battle. Without her, we would never return to the next meeting. Because of her, we can't not go.

I am beginning to realize that the more I fall, the more I am caught, that God puts clefts in the rocks. Whether we are climbing up, or falling down, the image works. There are places in the Rock of Ages where we can get what we want, but there aren't that many.

> *"We will know of God's presence by the very size of our frustrations. They signal our hope."*

If we are going to make it in the church—which is probably God's preference, if not also our own—then we will have to find more God, more clefts, more places to rest and renew. The important thing will be to make sure that we don't put doors on the clefts and close ourselves in. God will call us out, not in. God will provide the inner places so we can survive in the outer places; you just won't always know at what level of your climb the next one is going to appear.

We will know of God's presence by the very size of our frustrations. They signal our hope. When we stop having them, we have probably put a door on our hiding place, closed down, shut up. For some of us, the signal of our hope is anger. Why do we want so much from our churches and get so little? Why is our pastor or our moderator so terminally controlling? Who put so much fear in the Rock of Ages? Why do churches do so little for peace and justice when they could do so much? (I'll never forget the chair of a search committee a while back saying, "If you come here, I certainly hope you won't make too much of that peace and justice stuff." I never set foot in the place again.) Why does fear live where grace should abound? Are we foolish to want so much treasure from church or from one another?

> *"What galls me most about the church is the way it has substituted outer battles for inner ones."*

I think not. One of the ways the churches fail us is in their satisfaction with so little. Louise Bogan, the American poet, tells us:

> The certain method of stilling poetic talent is to substitute an outer battle for an inner one. A poet emerges from a spiritual crisis strengthened and refreshed only if she has been strong enough to fight it through at all levels, and at the deepest first. To avoid even the smallest crisis is to enter a world of bravada and leave the world of sincerity.

What galls me most about the church is the way it has substituted outer battles for inner ones. We pound on the table, adorned in the hypocrisy of the expensive suit, wanting nothing more than to continue the appearance of doing God's work. Very few churches actually want to do God's work; they/we pound the tables instead.

Because I know that the "insiders" experience this cynical faking as much as I do, I know that somehow my integrity issue parallels theirs. We are one at least in our frustration with the church, even if they name their frustration with my name, and I name mine with theirs.

I probably stay with the church because there are fewer and fewer places to take my longing for a good wrestling match with the poetry of our inner battles. I had thought church would be such a place, where we would be so hungry for justice and juice, music and dancing, that there would be no doubt about the depth of our fights. We would always know they would be about God and what God wanted through us in the world.

More of my battles are about whether we should serve cookies or sandwiches at the coffee hour. Or what to do with rambunctious children. Or who keeps the church kitchen cleaner, the "outsiders" or the "insiders." They have a very external, rather than internal, feel. And yet, who am I to tell God how to test me? These may be the battles of my longing. And it may be more up to me than I even realize to elevate and deepen these battles, so that the treasure hunt for God is of a piece with them. I know that I will be clefted along the way.

# CHAPTER TEN

> "For a while [the judge] refused; but later he said to himself,
> 'Though I have no fear of God and no respect for anyone, yet
> because this widow keeps bothering me, I will grant her
> justice, so that she may not wear me out by continually
> coming.'" (Luke 18:4-5)

# Hope in the Face of Death

*I* love the story of the persistent widow in Luke 18:1-8. She is one of my heroines. Against a cruel judge, she persists. She knows he is cruel, knows he doesn't want to give her justice, and yet she wears him down. By hounding him and harassing him and demanding of him justice, she gets it. Nothing delights me so as his giving in: "so that she may not wear me out by continually coming." I get hope every time I hear this story. Cruel judges can get weary. Injustice can wear down. Even evil gets tired.

Persistence is nothing if not hope with its working shoes on. Persistence is the daily, ordinary face of hope. You know what it takes to keep going against the odds. I know what it takes. It takes persistence to be persistent.

> *"We fear death and hope for Jesus—we have long expected them both."*

If we apply this virtue of persistence to the matter of our dying, some very interesting things happen. You may not see the connection immediately but you will if you use the lens of the hymn "Come, Thou Long Expected Jesus." Nothing is more expected than death. We all know it is coming, but we don't like to mention it every day. We all believe that Jesus is coming, but again, we don't dress that belief in its working shoes either. We fear death and hope for Jesus—we have long expected them both.

To face death with hope is to acknowledge the presence of Jesus in the moment of death. To face death with hope is to be ready, that beautiful way that most older people do get ready. They don't prepare for death so much as death prepares them for its coming. Sickness, fatigue, little bouts with their own mortality, each has a way of opening the heart to the fact of death. By the time people reach seventy, they have usually met their Maker in one hospital visit or car accident or another.

I have only to contrast the way young people drive cars—idiotically, with no expectation of mortality—and the way old people drive cars—carefully, slowly, painstakingly, with every expectation that something extraordinary may appear around the corner. We were playing tennis one night at our local park when a young man zoomed his motorcycle back and forth on the long, straight path, so fast that ears were splitting for blocks around. This young man was testing fate. He was having that young person's experience of limit bashing. It is hard when you are young to be aware that you are going to die. Everyone else has or will, and you will, too. But when you are young it doesn't feel that way. It is equally hard to be old and not know it.

The question of death is, rightly asked, the question of life. Not to be absorbed so much with the reality of death as to be absorbed with the matter of life. Okay, I am going to die. So what do I do now? How do I live now so that when I die, I die well?

A smart person once said to me that a biography, the story of a life, is actually the story of death. It ends, has a middle, and begins. But we write it down as a way to make sense of the person's life, but you can't get a really good biography until the person is dead. Then you can round it out.

This business of persisting toward justice, persisting toward Jesus, persisting toward God, is a very good way to live. It is an active embrace of death in that it says that Jesus is as much present at death as in life. Which is a fundamental assertion of Scripture. It is also a way of living in God's reality rather than worldly reality. In worldly reality, you live, you die, you pay taxes. In God's reality, there is this thing called eternity. You live, you die, you meet Jesus. What is on the other side no one knows. But the hopeful person expects—and long expects—that Jesus will be there in some form. The hopeful person expects a new beginning at death—doesn't know what it is or what it looks like—but is confident that, as life is good, so is death. Like the widow who didn't believe that the judge was really evil, but rather believed that she could get justice from him, we don't believe that death is evil. And if it is, or we begin to fear that it is, we simply wear our fear down.

All of these fine words about death and persisting toward Jesus in it are fine as long as the death is what we might call natural. As long as the person has had a good enough taste of life to lick the plate fairly clean. But when the death is premature, or involves a child, a whole other journey is required. The walk is not just hope with its working boots on. This walk is bare foot, calloused, much more the keeping on of the keeping on of the genuinely oppressed and God forsaken.

> "God's will may not be all powerful, but God's love is."

Some people always try to claim that every death is the "will" of God. I have never been able to believe that. I remember William Sloane Coffin speaking about the death of his nineteen-year-old son Alex. He died in a car crash. That kind where you knew the boy was doing his post-adolescent limit bashing and got caught. Coffin said that the only thing he could not endure were the letters coming from fellow clergy saying, "It was the will of God." He said there is no God who would take Alex. No such thing as a God who would do that.

If you talk to parents who have lost children, you will hear the battle with this theme over and over. They must battle this ancient theology just like the persistent widow did. The judge is unjust. But I mean to wear him down. My walking boots have worn out. My bare feet are killing me. But I mean to persist toward God, through Jesus, or toward meaning, through struggle, or even just toward life, if I can't bear any longer to speak the words *God* or *Jesus*. I mean to persist. I mean to long expect. I mean to keep on. The reason? I don't believe this was the will of God. I think there are some things that even God can't control.

The will of God is an overworked notion. Things may

happen outside the will of God. But nothing happens outside the love of God. God's will may not be all powerful, but God's love is.

This is a terribly important distinction. It is the theology of the cross. Surely if God's will were all powerful, God could have prevented the death of his own Son. But because God's will was bent on behalf of humanity, we see that evil has a pretty good contest with God. Even God doesn't know who is going to win, finally. But Paul says it so well, there is no point in saying it any differently, "Nothing can separate us from the love of God." Nothing. Not life, death, powers, principalities—or our widow would say—wicked judges. Nothing can separate us from the love of God. Therefore we persist toward Jesus, toward the light, toward the good, confident that even in death, there is goodness. Things may be out of control, even for God, but nothing can be without love.

This is why the persistent widow is such a good model as we approach our own deaths, or face the death of our loved ones. You keep on keeping on because love, not death, is final. You don't believe that the judge or that death or that evil can possibly win. And so you wear them down rather than let them wear you down.

G. K. Chesterton has a delightful set of images for this path of persistence. He was asked how he thought people kept being expectant in the face of death and difficulty. He answered, "They see a track in the snow, a lantern showing a path, a door set open." These images do seem to be the way. A track in the snow. You find that other people have made it through cold times, and so you hope that you can yourself. Or there is a lantern just at dusk or midnight or 3:00 A.M. In the long dark night of the soul, some unexpected light appears along the way, or—this one is my favorite—there is a door set open. Surely the persistent widow had little clues along the way. She saw the door set open. The judge didn't have the strength to beat her. He was weakening. She saw that the door was ajar, and she ran for it.

Many people confuse all of religion with this certainty of immortality, this definite belief in God's association and victory over human death. The words of William James seem important here. In his massive work, the *Varieties of Religious Experience,* he concludes in fear that he didn't spend enough time on immortality. He gives the reason for his neglect as "it is after all just a chance." I remember when I first read that. A chance? If immortality is just a chance, then what good is this long-expected Jesus, this cross, this hope, this faith? Now I see a little more of what he meant. Because he does continue. "No fact in human nature is more characteristic than its willingness to live on a chance. The existence of the chance makes the difference between a life of which the keynote is resignation and a life of which the keynote is hope." Do you see our friend the widow here? I do. She took the chance that she could wear the judge down. It would have been very easy for her to become resigned to his power. Just as it is very easy for us to become resigned to the power of death.

> *"We try to make this thing called hope grandiose when it is actually fairly small."*

If our child dies, our child dies. The child isn't there anymore. But, the widow would tell us, the meaning of the child's life remains. The love we felt remains. God's love remains.

There is a wonderful expression, "Forever and a day." I don't know where it comes from, but I know there is solace in it. As long as a child had one good sandbox or one good swing or one good dog, there was enough forever. Eternity is not out there, somewhere in the future, stretching endlessly in all directions. It's here, now, as a moment, as what is, a moment in eternity.

Sometimes we have such a hard time seeing a lot in a little that we fail ourselves and our own hope. We try to make this thing called hope grandiose when it is actually fairly small.

This penchant for the grandiose is everywhere. You can see it in the World Series, something that never really existed until the 1992 season when a Canadian team finally played. Or I saw it at the Farmer's Museum in Cooperstown one summer. Read the massive sign that greets you as you walk in there. "The New York State Historical Association welcomes you to the Farmers Museum at the Village Crossroads which shows how the plain people of yesterday in doing their daily work built a great nation where only a great forest had stood." The same grandiosity as the World Series in which only American cities vied until now. Where all they could see was a great forest in Cooperstown—and it galls me that it is the New York State Historical Association, who should know better, saying these things—there had been natives since 33,000 B.C. Between A.D. 1350 and 1600 five nations of the Iroquois were there. In chapter 3 of James Fenimore Cooper's great book *Deerslayer*, there is a lovely statement about Council Rock, that "it was well known to all the indians in that part of the country."

Why am I pointing out these grandiosities while talking about the long-expected Jesus? Because I think one way to be hopeful in the face of our deaths is to right-size it. As H. L. Mencken puts it in a file left for those who followed him, the file marked obituary, "don't overdo it."

You will die. I will die. Our children, God forbid, may die before their time. But not one of these matters is the end of the world. The Iroquois tribes lost children and survived. The good things of life abide. Hot fudge will still be there. Council Rock will still be there. Fall leaves will still turn to glory. Motorcycles will still be there. Many will persist toward God, away from evil, long after we are gone.

> *Many will persist toward God, away from evil, long after we are gone.*

Or for a more humorous approach to the entire matter, we could just stay home and read the new book called *The Decline and Fall of Practically Everybody.* This thing called death is the instigator of hope!

There is no need to belittle the pain of lost children while speaking the words of hope. We must endure pain and have hope, simultaneously. Surely there is awful grief to endure.

I remember being on a subway once in France when a crowd of gypsies got on the train. Maybe ten children, two women. One bumped me rather vigorously, and then in a sneering voice, said, "Pardoneme." Everyone on the train locked her purse because it is well known that the gypsies pickpocket as a way of living. Since the break up of the old Europe, the gypsies are even more desperately condemned to travel. Two of the girls about age ten left the group to wander up and down the car, singing a sardonic song, begging, and insulting people for money. They moved to the next car, apparently to do the same thing. As they moved out of the train on their way to the next car, they couldn't get the doors open to the car. The train pulled away, leaving

the two girls stranded there. The scream, "*Mamma,*
*Mamma,*" reverberated through the station as the train
pulled out.

I don't know if the drama was intended or not. What I
do know is that it was drama. Children abandoned. Moth-
ers losing children in a great subway station in a great city.

I was with my seven-year-old son. We made a deal that if
ever we got separated in the Metro, we each would get off
at the very next stop and wait there for the other. Jacob
found great comfort in this notion of waiting and being
found.

When a child dies, it is like missing your stop. You don't
make your total journey. It is interrupted. Nothing is harder for a pastor, I know, than having to do the funeral services of people who get off the train before their time, at
the wrong stop. The reason is the fear that such evil may
be the will of God. It is not. God is there at the stop, with
love for the one abandoned. We will get to the next stop
ourselves. We can hope to meet them there. Or at least we
can live our life with the promise that we will try to do just
that. That our love, our protection, our being with, will
endure.

Come, thou long-expected Jesus. Come as a track in the
snow. Or a lantern showing a path. Or a door set open. Be
there when we get off our stop. We will persist toward you
even as we know you persist toward us. Wait for us, as we
wait for you. And wait with our children.

# CHAPTER ELEVEN

*All of them were filled with the Holy Spirit and began to speak in other languages, as the Spirit gave them ability.*
*(Acts 2:4)*

# Hope to Get High

*D*id you ever wonder how a bird finds food in the winter? If you stand and watch, you'll notice wild creatures often seem to look for food in deep crevices, almost anywhere, especially on tree bark.

Many of us are capable of deep caring for animals. We love our pets. We can be tender about the need of a bird but fear even commenting on own hungers. Even fewer of us have the capacity to care for the human poor as much as we can care for small animals.

I like to use animals in my preaching and pastoring as a way of prying open the shells of those who come to me for help. I use my own animals as a way of opening up a little myself. Sitting by a cat in the evening, or petting the boisterous dog upon returning home, is just as relaxing to me as it is to nursing home patients who are now widely reported as being helped by animal contact.

The best laugh I've had lately is from a woman whose poodle went along with her to a friend's house and jumped into the pool when she jumped into the pool. The whole idea made me forget a little of myself. What a relief. We have a good laugh—and hope that the poodle can swim. By the way, it could. It was the poodle's owner who couldn't swim with the poodle in her arms.

> *"How was anybody ever going to understand how much you can love an old fleabag of a cat who has a phantom brother?"*

Bring up the subject of animals and almost everybody has a story, a warmth, a sense of amplitude. I once had a cat named Ringo Starr who left my farm in Pennsylvania to move to New York. Really. He found small-town life much too regulating. His brother, Sargent Pepper, stayed behind and mourned his brother's decision almost daily. Sargent Pepper had to manage all the mice in the barn, as well as all the adults in the family. Imagine having the responsibility for all the laps! Many cats are like this one in being given too much responsibility at too early an age. Perhaps that is why this cat learned to start at one end of the house and run to pick up speed, jump on the screen door, and use his momentum to cast himself out into the yard.

He also slept under the covers, next to my feet. When he died, I was beside myself for days, and I didn't really know how to tell anyone about it. I thought they would laugh at me for loving that cat too much. I thought the discerning among them would figure out that I had split my personality between these two cats, and that now both of them were gone. How could I tell them what all we had been through together, how many of the nights he had warmed my feet when I had cried myself to sleep? How could I tell them about the many times the only reason I could think of to pull myself together was that the cat needed something? How could I explain how often I had used him as an excuse to stay alive? How was anybody ever going to understand how much you can love an old fleabag of a cat who has a phantom brother?

Take my local clergy luncheon. One pastor announced her upcoming divorce, after a short marriage. Another announced her engagement; she had made this announcement twice before. A third spoke of how his integrity demanded that he resign as the new associate at a church that just fired its old pastor. A fourth said his church was seriously closing its doors six months from now. A fifth had just survived a vote on his leadership— 140 for him, 82 against. A sixth had been reprimanded by her deacons for speaking on war and peace. They had given her "guidelines." A seventh was brand new in his pulpit and was surprised to discover that there were rules for the use of the parsonage. There were only eight of us there. I made jokes about my cats because I was too stunned to do otherwise.

> *"Each of us gets to that middle time, that time after Easter, after knowing that we are saved, when we could use a visitation of the holy."*

There is a little bit of winter bird in every one of us. We have a long hunt for our food every day. The poor have routine desperation that they are ashamed to discuss. But each of us gets to that middle time, that time after Easter, after knowing that we are saved, when we could use a visitation of the holy. Pentecost comes to break in the middle, to provide a crevice from which to feed. Once fed, we become capable of sustaining our commitments, even if that means jumping into the pool, even if it means telling someone else what hurts, even if it means staying high while others are low.

Most people don't have my cat's courage. Lots of people deal with the regulation of small-town, middle-class, middle aged, middle-of-the-road life by fantasy. Romance novels, bourbon, or beer becomes the fantasy by which we move to the Greenwich Village in our mind.

The gospel doesn't condemn cats who take off for the city. The gospel doesn't condemn our urgency for a little bit of high, of self-transcendence and forgetfulness. Rather than condemn these urgings in us, the gospel rewards them by suggesting that they, rather than our routines, are normal.

> ## "The story of Pentecost is a strategy for winter feeding."

The story of Pentecost is a strategy for winter feeding, a strategy for renewing a life that has gotten stuck in its own regularity. So many people think of the gospel of Jesus Christ as assistance in keeping your nose to the grindstone. And that it is. But the way the gospel assists us in keeping our noses to the grindstones is to allow us a singular freedom from those grindstones. It says that even though Jesus is gone, Jesus is here. At their worst moment, the disciples got high on their own faith.

You can see the Pentecost in a person by the difference between light and darkness in their eyes—their sparkle, the way they walk, the way they talk. You can see the Pentecost in whether or not their language is one of possibility—sure, we can do that—or impossibility—you can't do that. That can't be done.

Pentecost is precisely the sparkle in a person, the evidence of a holier spirit carrying them, the evidence of a lightness, a little space that is open to the animal, to the smaller delights, to the unnecessary caress of a cat, or unnecessary delight of observing a bird at breakfast.

Pentecost is a way of looking at birds and knowing that they will be fed for the winter. It is a way of laughing at a poodle who jumps into a pool straight into the arms of someone whom he thought loved him. Pentecost is a way of keeping commitments long after the weather has become cold. It is a way to get high rather than a way to survive being low. Pentecost is a hope that some of the new wine will come your way; or, barring that, that you will find a way to eat and be satisfied in winter.